10 MISSISSIPPI

10 Mississippi

POEMS

STEVE HEALEY

COFFEE HOUSE PRESS

MINNEAPOLIS

2010

COFFEE HOUSE PRESS books are available to the trade through our primary distributor, Consortium Book Sales & Distribution, www.cbsd.com or (800) 283-3572. For personal orders, catalogs, or other information, write to: info@coffeehousepress.org.

Coffee House Press is a nonprofit literary publishing house. Support from private foundations, corporate giving programs, government programs, and generous individuals helps make the publication of our books possible. We gratefully acknowledge their support in detail in the back of this book.

To you and our many readers around the world,
we send our thanks for your continuing support.

LIBRARY OF CONGRESS CIP INFORMATION

Healey, Steve

10 Mississippi : poems / Steve Healey. — 1st ed.

p. cm.

ISBN 978-1-56689-252-0 (alk. paper)

I. Title.   II. Title: Ten Mississippi.

PS3608.E238A613 2010

811'.6—DC22

PRINTED IN THE UNITED STATES

1 3 5 7 9 8 6 4 2

FIRST EDITION | FIRST PRINTING

ENORMOUS THANKS:

—to all my family, friends, students, and colleagues.

—to those who generously read and responded to earlier versions of this manuscript: Jessica Knight, William Waltz, Dobby Gibson, and Sarah Fox.

—to everyone whose words, art, and actions helped inspire these poems, including: Nico Healey, Clark Astor Waltz, Randall Heath, John Colburn, and Kevin Carollo.

—to the following magazines for publishing some of these poems: *Boston Review; Forklift, Ohio; H_NGM_N; Jellyroll; jubilat; Pool; Post Road.*

—to Alison Morse, from Talking Image Connection, for inviting me to write and read poetry in response to Frontier Preachers (an installation art show exploring the history of the Mississippi River), on display in the summer of 2009 at the Soap Factory in Minneapolis. That poetry eventually became "10 Mississippi," the ten-part poem contained in this book.

—to the intrepid and supportive leaders of my favorite literary organizations, including: Chris Fischbach, Molly Mikolowski, Linda Koutsky, and Allan Kornblum of Coffee House Press; Eric Lorberer and Kelly Everding of *Rain Taxi Review of Books;* and William Waltz and Brett Astor of *Conduit* magazine.

for Jessie and Nico

ONE

TWO

THREE

FOUR

FIVE

SIX

One

IN REGARD TO THE WILDNESS of birds towards man, there is no way of accounting for it, except as an inherited habit: comparatively few young birds, in any one year, have been injured by man in England, yet almost all, even nestlings, are afraid of him; many individuals, on the other hand, both at the Galapagos and at the Falklands, have been pursued and injured by man, but yet have not learned a salutary dread of him. We may infer from these facts, what havoc the introduction of any new beast of prey must cause in a country, before the instincts of the indigenous inhabitants have become adapted to the stranger's craft or power.

—CHARLES DARWIN,
The Voyage of the Beagle, *1845*

THERE IS NOTHING STRANGE about the fact that lambs bear a grudge towards large birds of prey: but that is no reason to blame the large birds of prey for carrying off the little lambs. And if the lambs say to each other, "These birds of prey are evil; and whoever is least like a bird of prey and most like its opposite, a lamb,—is good, isn't he?", then there is no reason to raise objections to this setting-up of an ideal beyond the fact that the birds of prey will view it somewhat derisively, and will perhaps say, "We don't bear any grudge at all towards these good lambs, in fact we love them, nothing is tastier than a tender lamb."

—FRIEDRICH NIETZSCHE,
On the Genealogy of Morality, 1887

Lifeboat, Wingspan

When I build a city on the Mississippi,
there's an egret gliding through the air.
She crosses the river then circles back
and lands on a piece of sunlight.
In my city, many buildings surround the egret.
Many clouds sit on the buildings.
There are many ways to predict the weather.
When my head feels light, it rains on Monday.
When the sun returns, the phone rings.
It's my sister saying hello. She's putting
a bullet in my brain. There's no time
for twilight. Or a certain pill has my name
on it, but there's no time to swallow.
I'm on a balcony looking at the Mississippi
like a pill with nowhere to go.
Once I was the luckiest bird in the world
and still I wanted to be something else.
I wanted to be a weightless architect
who finds her mirrored windows on fire.
Once it was a Monday, and I was an egret
holding my red glass breath, not knowing
how to be burned alive. Someone said,
we need water to put out the fire. Soon
water became scarce, water was the new oil.
We remembered how it used to rain.
Each dot on the street was a new idea
until all the dots became one big wet.
Now it's Monday, and when I see an egret,
my tongue flattens. A white stain waves
good-bye very slowly. I hear a voice

on the phone. It's my sister saying hello.
When I deny having a sister, the sun
burns her skin. When I deny it's spring,
rain begins to fall. When twilight arrives,
my city on the Mississippi begins to
disappear. I wave good-bye to the egret.
I'm ready for the pluvial air.

New Fighting Technologies

A rock can be used as a weapon.
Paper can wrap around the rock
and suffocate it. Scissors can come along
and cut the paper into little pieces,
and we can throw ourselves at the scissors
like a rock. A person can be used
as a weapon. A person can be hurt
by a weapon. The sun can fall on our heads
and make us want to fight for darkness.
Every day it's a war to end daylight.
After the early fog lifts, God gets parched,
the death toll is called "unacceptable."
The average heart beats a billion and a half
times per life. Every day shadows wrap
around the planet like black paper,
and new soldiers receive a signing bonus.
There's a cost to replacing day with night.
Ever since Saint Michael slayed that dragon
named Satan with a human sword,
humans have been used as weapons
with increasing effectiveness.
Not a day ends without the sun
totally surrendering. It's always
the same last light that touches the faces
of new casualties lying in their own blood.
Now we can put the kids to bed
with the same good story. Sleep tight,
don't let the bed bugs eat your face,
don't let the doors get blown away.
Night is out there waiting to hurt us,

even after saving us from daylight.
Night makes soldiers feel invisible.
They wear naked uniforms, they dream
about saying something really stupid,
they wake up feeling belligerent.
Thus the casus belli. We dream
of naked soldiers with soft skin,
having lost the ability to be awake.
We're stiff as the dead, stiff enough
to work eight hours while dreaming
of being casual. We sit there
searching for the right words
to make the final weapon
that will force the sun to set.
Finally we say the words,
the sun is setting.
And then we wait.

Ketchup over the Park

shall never vanquished be until / Great Birnam
wood to high Dunsinane hill / Shall come
—SHAKESPEARE, *Macbeth*

We who crossed so many bridges to be in this park,
to hear the hugely amplified music and to support the troops,
they who are like hamburger meat receiving support
from the eaters of grilled beef patties, we who
fire up a million grills in the shade of the ketchup factory,
who know that its neon red bottle will never cease to flash,

Lord, we are not worthy of your flavor, but we have come
from so many directions, we have crossed rivers with monsters
in them, we have felt like a perfect Frisbee toss,
that lightness when you first start over a bridge and think,
my God, that river is so far below, I am being delivered
from evil, I make a sign of the cross, I acknowledge
that people die, but I also acknowledge that ketchup exists,
you have to put it on top of the meat, never on the bottom,
so it rises to the roof of your mouth, the sugary tang
enters your sinuses, your brain flashes good red music,

it's so good that you know some enemy must be coming,
like an enigmatic prophesy, and we notice that some of us
are wearing tree costumes, suspicion mounts, we know
that Macbeth is going to get fucked, and it is we who
will do the fucking, we who will eat the hamburgers
and say good-bye, this war is ended.

Intelligent Design

> *Value, therefore, does not stalk about*
> *with a label describing what it is. It*
> *is value, rather, that converts every*
> *product into a social hieroglyphic.*
> *Later on, we try to decipher the*
> *hieroglyphic, to get behind the secret of*
> *our own social products; for to stamp*
> *an object of utility as a value, is just as*
> *much a social product as language.*
> —KARL MARX, *Capital*

She sells seashells by the seashore.
She earns minimum wage selling
sex toys in the form of seashells,
harpoons, sextants, ships in bottles, etc.
In the shiny seashore sunshine she sells
the secret fetishism of commodities,
satisfaction guaranteed. Protected
by SPF 30 sunscreen, she sells
the idea of having sex with centuries
of salty seafarers, not the sex itself
but the secret saltiness that causes
shoppers to salivate. Her voice slips
into the ear of every shopper
telling them that inside each seashell
the sea is having sex with its shore,
and by extension, with every shopper
on that shore. Therefore, they must
be prepared to have the best sex
using the best sex toys. Therefore,
she sells a sea full of problems

18

and solutions intelligently designed
by the one true supernatural designer.
Each design is part of a grand design
that remains a secret, protected by
intellectual property laws. Therefore,
she sells maritime erotica produced
across the sea in factories that she
cannot see. Therefore, she sells
distance. The secret distance inside
intimacy. The idea of watching
a pirate have sex with a ship's captain
for her entire eight-hour shift.
The pirate begins to look like
her best friend from grade school
who always rode the red seahorse
on the carousel down by the seashore.
She had forgotten this best friend
so completely, he is like a messiah
coming back from the dead, riding
the captain as if he were a red seahorse.
The messiah tells her that in exchange
for her sins she will suffer by working
eight-hour shifts until she dies.
Then, according to the grand design,
she'll become a pirate and ride
whichever seahorse on the carousel
she likes, forever and ever.

Animals among Us

Night is when we say it's night.
It's night and we're in the backyard.
In the backyard we gaze at the slug.
We say the slug slimes the chard.
On a large leaf of chard it makes
a slimy path. We say the path is errant,
like a song getting lost. We say day
is already lost, or night took the colors
of day and poured them onto Asia.
The slug is like a small shiny elephant
without legs, longing for Asia.
Night cannot include day, we say.
That's the law, the final black
that comes after dusk. We say night
cannot love everything. If the slug
loves an elephant and penetrates it,
we say the crow is excluded.
The crow eats trash in the alley
and talks a black speech about not
being loved. We say only the future
loves the crow flying into late summer.
Sometimes August is there, and there
is meat rotting in the heat, meat that
loves the crow. There is the memory
of animals who were recently alive,
a hot sky, lightning without thunder,
and now. Now is a life we live
now, benighted in the backyard,
forgetting that birds exist, because
now there are crickets clashing

in the dying grass. August of
re-enacting famous Civil War battles,
August of forgetting the pain
of benighted heroes. It's the easiest thing
in the world to live during the time
of dying crickets, unless you are
another animal feeling excluded
from the massacre. We say this is how
they chirr in the dark, we say August
is dedicated to the proposition
that all lawns are created, now
we are engaged in a great cricket war,
testing whether that nation, or any nation,
can long endure accumulating dew.
Those who are hurt will be nursed
by their own ghosts. The slug will be
removed from the hole in the elephant
and placed once again on the chard,
to enjoy a slow pleasant death.
We say the chard will be good for dinner,
sautéed in a little white wine.

The Invention of the Alphabet,
or The Quick Brown Fox Jumps
over the Lazy Dog

I sit at the front of the school bus and see the fox as it slips under the wheel. There's a loud squeal and crunch. The bus drives on as if nothing happened.

Yesterday Mrs. Berger taught us a sentence that contains every letter of the alphabet. She said, don't repeat this sentence or else something awful may happen.

Her name is a food that I like to eat with ketchup. Her lips have a lot of red on them. She said, imagine what you can do with all those letters.

I know that the bus is a big yellow throat. That's why I don't sit in the back. In the front you can see three seconds from now. You can go deep inside your ears and not hear a sound.

Mrs. Berger said, some things are real and some are not. Some things are sad and some are happy. Some people never close their eyes, some people never sleep. The fox and the dog are more real than us because they know every word.

I know it's my fault that the fox is dead. When we get to school, I'm first off the bus. Twenty-six letters are lined up waiting to kick my ass.

I close my eyes and send all the letters into a tree. It's Christmas, and they look like ornaments. Z sits on the top branch, looking down on the whole world.

On the sidewalk there's a lazy dog curled up like baby Jesus. I jump over him.

TWO

In a blinding fog, 100 laments wash upon a beach.

—LANGUAGE REMOVAL SERVICES,
Ecstatic Opera Vol. 1: The 100 Headless Diva

IT WAS CHARACTERISTIC of the inner detachment he had hitherto so successfully cultivated and to which our whole account of him is a reference, it was characteristic that his complications, such as they were, had never yet seemed so as at this crisis to thicken about him, even to the point of making him ask himself if he were, by any chance, of a truth, within sight or sound, within touch or reach, within the immediate jurisdiction, of the thing that waited.

—HENRY JAMES, *The Beast in the Jungle*

While I Held My Breath Underwater

That afternoon I was listening to a record of Adelina Patti
singing Bellini's famous aria, "Casta Diva."
I had been attempting to plot her voice on a graph,
but its nuances kept evading my calculations,
and my attention eventually revisited my childhood efforts
to hold my breath underwater for long durations.
Apparently I'd convinced myself that within my held breath
I could access secret rooms or small pairs of lungs
that allowed me to breathe while, in fact, not breathing.
Of course, I did not need to be underwater to hold my breath,
but apparently, such was the indisputable evidence
I needed to prove that I was not, in fact, breathing.
In any case, this particular method of not breathing
was accompanied by a peculiar sound—akin to silence
but not silence itself, perhaps a silence so total that it allows
one finally to hear oneself—and that's when I realized
that the needle was skipping at the end of the record.

The aria was over, Adelina Patti's exquisitely lilting voice
no longer singing to me, but rather than reaching out
my hand and returning the needle to the beginning,
I sat there, unable to move, absorbing each pop and sweep
of static—the sound, as it were, of Adelina's absence.
I was strangely content, perhaps more content than
I'd ever been, despite my knowing how difficult it is
to measure contentedness accurately. I felt a sense
of having gone beyond, having let go of certain limits,
and yet it occurred to me that I had forgotten to eat
my lunch. Earlier I had purchased a Filet-O-Fish
with the clear intention of eating it, but at that moment

I was quite certain that I had not eaten it. I had no memory
of my tongue penetrating that warm salty breading,
my saliva mixing with the tangy tartar sauce.
I remembered, in other words, that I had forgotten to eat,
which meant that I should have been hungry,
but in fact I was not hungry. I was perfectly content
to let that cold square of deep-fried fish rest in peace
in its little coffin of congealed vegetable oil.
It seemed to me that I might be content to never move
again, to be forever with this sound of the needle
skipping, forever in Adelina's aftermath.

That's when it occurred to me that my listening
to the needle skipping might be an event that I was
in fact remembering while holding my breath underwater.
In other words, my being underwater might have lead me
back to an earlier time when I had sat contentedly
in Adelina's aftermath, remembering her lilting voice.
This was precisely my thought at that moment, although I knew
how difficult it would be to determine conclusively
which event was the present and which the remembered.
If I were indeed underwater at the present moment,
it would certainly be possible to see some fish swim by
on occasion. In fact, I might want to befriend those fish
as fellow denizens of this subaqueous realm,
and just as this thought occurred to me I realized
why I had neglected to eat my Filet-O-Fish.
Not merely a lapse of memory, it had been a gesture
of compassion, or more accurately, guilt for having colluded
in the death of one of my own gilled companions.

I remembered, moreover, that my mother had never
allowed me to enter the water directly after a meal,
lest I develop a debilitating postprandial cramp,
which perhaps further explained why I had bypassed
lunch altogether. By contrast, that same woman
whom I called my mother had never voiced concern
about my attempts to hold my breath underwater.
Although I looked for signs of maternal concern
repeatedly, and repeatedly pushed my lung capacity
and life to the fatal edge, she appeared indifferent
about the very real possibility of my drowning.
In fact, she occasionally said with a smile that drowning
would make me the greatest breath-holder ever.
Of course, this was true—there could be no truer statement,
and as a breath-holder determined to succeed,
I needed to reckon with this truth, for any breath-holder
who survives to breathe another breath has, to some degree,
failed. At that moment I could hear those words clearly
issuing from her smiling mouth, as if she were present,
or present in voice despite being absent in body.

And yet that voice, too, sounded somewhat removed,
as if I were listening to a message my mother had left
on my voice mail, a message that I had listened to
at some later point in time—minutes later or years later,
I don't remember. First came the voice of the voice mail,
a woman I do not know telling me that I do indeed
have exactly one message waiting for me. Then came
the message itself, definitely the voice of my mother,
or probably, I should say, for the voice did have
a scratchy, muffled quality, almost ghostly at times.
And to be honest, the words of the message seemed
to have been removed, as if the voice-mail lady had

given me the option of deleting the words themselves
and listening to whatever mouth noises remained.
Nonetheless, despite having no linguistic content,
that voice did seem to be speaking familiar things to me,
as if I were underwater and my mother were speaking
to me from some nearby shore. Gazing up through
the water's shimmering surface, I saw what I thought
to be her wavy outline, the smiling mouth moving
as if speaking, as if providing some important content.
Was she telling me to continue holding my breath
a little longer? I could not say for sure, for as I have said,
what I heard was a sort of ghostly and edited version
of the original, if one can say that any voice has an origin.

What I can say with certainty is that just under the surface
of that voice I began to hear a needle skipping, as if
at the end of a record that continued to spin around
and around, and that this was the key piece of evidence,
indeed the proof that Adelina had come back to me
from Bellini's "Casta Diva." I knew then that it was her,
or more precisely, her voice, that had made me,
that had fed me in the absence of so many lunches,
and that it was for her that I would keep striving
to be the greatest underwater breath-holder
the world has ever known.

Three

I do not want to be a person.

—ANNE CARSON,
    "Stanzas, Sexes, Seductions"

Moreover, you must walk like a camel

—HENRY DAVID THOREAU,
    "Walking"

What if There Is a Person

who walks in my sneakers
on the clean sidewalks of this town?
Not knowing where to go but present
enough to hear the crunch of an ant
that he unintentionally steps on.
A person who stays on the official
concrete paths can kill without
much fear of being stepped on
or beaten by a stick. Here comes
the new pedestrian bridge that looks
like a hand being pulled slowly apart,
pinkie and thumb going east and west,
the hand of a person widely believed
to exist, to be at large, a prime
suspect in killer sneakers. A person
who smells like me, like sweat
and cinnamon gum. Who recalls
my past toothaches and yet refuses
to look at me when I speak to him.
Who is therefore always being
interrogated, walking a sidewalk
around an interrogator's eyes,
anticipating the next question.
Do you see a person whose mouth
is speaking to you? Dear person,
how are you? I have a drought
in my eyes. This town has forgotten
how to rain. I'm walking too slowly
toward any one ocean. As a nomad
or whale, I'm nearly extinct. As

a mail carrier, I screen your mail.
I have less and less to lose, my body
will be found in a septic tank.
Therefore I love you with my whole
starvation. I give you this leaf
that controls everything.

A Bay in Big Sur

The plan is to let the ocean do its thing.
The ocean's thing is to keep reaching for the shore.

There's no holding on. The fog is here and not here.
The bay's idea of whiteness tries to hold on.

The brain follows the curve of bay. A baby staggers
under a huge hat. The surf sucks on baby's toes.

This is how it comes to an end. Never has the ocean
so gently come to nothing. Not like how it slaps

and slaps the church-sized rock in the bay.
The rock is being punished. Birds have been shitting

on it for years. How much guano does it take to turn
a rock white? How much whiteness does it take

to hide behind fog? But we feel close to the rock.
We love it for sitting there covered in guano.

It has no plan except to let the birds keep doing
their thing. It tells us that we can let go of our brains.

We don't need to solve for the sum of X and Y.
We can pretend to be dead. We can be a bunch of skin

letting the sun lick us clean. In fact, many of us
are lying facedown in the sand, shot through the brain.

Many of us are happy to soak the sand with our blood,
no longer employed as planners, living no plan

to its logical end. The place where X is the trigger
and Y is the brain finally relaxing, employed now

by the air. Now two pelicans land on the shitty rock.
Pensive and heavy, they make nothing happen.

The fish make them hungry just by existing.
There is hunger that doesn't go away. There are

waves that never get to break to become news
of the broken. The baby is not breaking under

the weight of the huge hat. The baby's flesh
waits silently under his sweet white skin.

Appositive

This is the word that I can never remember.
Although I know it means "a name that renames,"
the word itself remains in the shadows like a panther.
Perhaps it is me who creates that distance,
describing the panther in what seems like plain language:
"its coat is golden and spotted with black rosettes."
Then I'm required to ask, what is a rosette?
A flower, a fact of the body, and another black noun
that requires renaming. May I take a rosette
from that panther and give it to you? Then what
do you do if you are a daylily? Why have that name?
Because you are "a showy, trumpet-shaped flower"
who says, "this is a day." Thus a name spreads
from the garden to a network of alleys that has no center.
From above, you can see that you're a panther
in the network, a panther lapping rainwater
from the lid of a garbage can, a panther the size
of a garbage truck, letting go of thirst, letting
the world go down its throat. Its tail curls into a question,
what is this? What's my name? Am I really a dog
with white spots, a dog named Spot, a dog
who hates panthers? I have learned that only one animal
means to protect me, the other means to kill me.
One star gives me a wish, the other is an airplane
that can go anywhere. From up there, I can see
a network of alleys, I can see that tomorrow will be

another nice day to be a daylily. I don't remember
how to be night-colored, but tonight is a nice night
for the ghosts to come back as black clouds
and pencil shavings and all the black words
I've erased. The rain is a reminder.

A Man without a Mouth

A man is about to die. He lies in a hammock.
He is afraid of death and the terrible heat of hell.
He is afraid of being judged by hell's omniscient birds.
He is afraid of being flung into the Cascade Mountains
wearing a pair of Rossignols. He slaloms
down the slope and thinks, this is not hell at all.
This is not the warm shit of time in a fluorescent cell,
this is not the mouth of a volcano lined with baby teeth.
The cold wind makes his eyes weep little icicles,
and he accidentally drops one of his poles. Soon
the chairlift attendant guides him back into the hammock,
and the sun slips behind a billboard to shade his eyes.
On the billboard is a huge tube of Pepsodent and a woman
with a white smile. The man thinks that his teeth
have always wanted to escape from his mouth,
and that he brushes them as punishment for being disloyal.
He thinks his dentist plays music that denies the existence
of pain, and that white is the color of pain because
it is accused of not being a color. He thinks that
over time he grows whiter, and that when the end
comes, it will be a perfect whiteness, a pure pain.
He knows that we have been watching him,
and that we can see his eyes twitch as it begins to snow.
He begins to pray for the return of his lost ski pole,
but it has already found him. We wonder if the man
has ever really been honest with us. We watch
the blood soak his white shirt, then we fly away.

Global Capitalism

*All the elements of corruption and exploita-
tion are imposed on us by the linguistic and
communicative regimes of production:
destroying them in words is as urgent as
doing so in deeds.*
—MICHAEL HARDT & ANTONIO NEGRI,
Empire

I would have said it in fewer words
if there were fewer things
coming to my piehole
asking to be included.
"No" is one word I could
have said more often. No,
this tea party cannot accommodate you,
elephant. I've already invited turkey,
bee, fish, wolf, and platypus,
and my igloo is about to burst.
Yet what I said kept growing,
the facts of my ice world
grew more fluid. In fact,
it started to rain, I started to smell
wet bodies, and what made me human
grew an elephantine desire.
Finally, no more family secrets,
except how we were all conceived
and what began at conception
beyond the desire to add
to the conversation without
sounding stupid or dead.
Is that such a crime? Well,

no need for apologies. I too
have invested unwisely in the future.
There will be plenty of pain
for those who can afford it.

The Spider Who Loved
the World Too Much

There is a web whose spider is dead.
There is a spider who dangles from the web
that stretches from the house to the lilac hedge.
There are threads that cling only where necessary,
in case a freak breeze cuts through this breezeless heat.
There is an electric grid straining because it loves
to destroy the heat before a cold front comes in.
It loves that the spider is so dead she can't even feel
the record high temperature of this Tuesday in June.
It is a good day to do nothing but sit on the porch
sweating on the newspaper, eating cold sweaty grapes
without knowing that there is a spider who loved you
to death. If you could return the spider's love,
you could see the way that face dangles upside down,
facing the fire hydrant that stands on the curb.
The red of the hydrant looks like a crazy fire,
and there is water inside waiting to destroy the red.
If you could follow that water back to the river
like a dead face that never stops loving you,
the way the river never stops loving its gulf,
you could follow it back to a computer model
of the cold front coming in. They say on Wednesday
two fronts will fall in love violently, but now cars
still pass in a Tuesday way, and the walkers walk
like endangered beasts or modern nation-states
looking for something to hate that actually exists.
It's hard to hate what doesn't exist, but you
have to love the walkers anyway. They sweat
in more places and each one silently tells

a fabulous fable about the love of just going,
the love of no longer dangling but walking across
a webby kingdom, coming back to life.

The Laws of Raining

*to assume among the powers of the earth, the
separate and equal station to which the Laws
of Nature and of Nature's God entitle them*
—THE DECLARATION OF INDEPENDENCE

If you are rain, eventually your training wheels
must come off, you must learn to fall freely.
It's natural to progress and become independent,
but if you fail, it's against the law to cry about it.
Crybabies will be burned by the police.
Those who precipitate correctly will live wet lives.
Those unwilling to be free will show signs of illness.
Sneezes come in pairs, like training wheels,
to remind you that you are not completely free.
If only one sneeze comes out of you, the other is lost,
and being lost is a freedom from being found.
It's true that losers are weepers, and finders keep
living a life without pain. One good mother
is all it takes to keep pushing the morphine button.
One good mother is all you need to exist.
It's natural to drink from a pair of breasts
without the ability to speak or ride a bicycle.
Alphabet blocks are like training wheels for words.
To spell the name of your god, first you must exist.
You need to be built around a spine, then climb
down the vertebrae into the valley of your piss.
That's where the founding fathers live,
naturally making laws and writing them down,
because one good law is worth a thousand fathers.
If you stay out all night, don't come home.

One good police baton can fuck up your spine.
To go to heaven, you must have the freedom
beaten out of you. Clouds gather to beat
cats and dogs out of heaven. If you catch
a tiger by the toe, your mother says to pick
the very best one, and you are not it,
you are the best rain ever.

Green Shoes

If you're looking for my knees,
they can be found halfway up my legs.
They are not pretty. They resemble
piggy banks that have been broken
and glued back together several times.
Yet they are useful. When I walk,
they allow my tibias to swing
slightly ahead of me into the future.
My feet take turns landing
on a new piece of ground up ahead.
My feet are wearing green shoes,
and when I walk, the grass grows.
I watch how effective the grass is
at growing, except that I'm a liar,
in fact the grass is dying.
It has not rained for weeks
and the grass is now a brown mat.
I think about the other crimes
I could commit. I could kick
a hole in a pony and take all
the gold doubloons that fall out.
Sometimes I walk to that place
where the cop stands in front
of the yellow tape and say,
what happened, officer?
The cop says something but
all I can hear is a child crying.
It sounds like coins hitting the street.
That's when I know it's time
to escape. My knees go into action.

I'm walking again. I'm wearing
the ghosts of green cows on my feet,
and they make all the difference.

Against Violence

The idea that to get at the thing without disturbing it,
the thing articulated in its natural juices,
the idea that the thing waits there to be thought,
the animal that plays dead or sleeps
knowing that soon the idea will come,
or will think it has come,

to get at the thing in its home country,
where it can naturally be found, it's a citizen
of the country whose time has come to be violent,
the idea of violence for the good of the thing,
the idea that every state in the country has another name
for it—the Natural State, the Sunshine State,
the state where they make weapons
to protect the thing, that which destroys
the future cause of destruction,

the idea that thinks it has a body,
the job of the body to crave salt, the job of salt
to dissolve in the mouth, the idea that after a long day
the ice cream man is empty, saltless,
he can no longer name a patriotic frozen confection
except to commit an act of violence against it,

in fact he could kill a confection in front of a child,
causing that child to be frozen in a state
of waiting for another sweet thing to come—
tomorrow's heat, for example, which is itself
an idea waiting for a frozen confection
to come and destroy it,

so a thing enters the hot mouth of the child,
the sweet colors of the country come
as a sudden violent coolness, the idea of the country
coloring the child's lips, the thing that can't be
thought yet, not until the time comes to be violent,

like thunder is an idea thought by lightning,
or the salted ocean that comes to take away
the ice cream man, because the day has been long,
many more people will be killed before tomorrow,
the idea has already come, it has been paid for,
and if you are a citizen of the country,
it is time to sleep.

Four

THE HUMAN BABY PROTECTS itself by means of *repetition* (the same fairy tale, one more time, or the same game, or the same gesture). Repetition is understood as a protective strategy in the face of the shock caused by new and unexpected experiences. So, the problem looks like this: is it not true that the experience of the baby is transferred into adult experience, into the prevalent forms of behavior at the center of the great urban aggregates . . . ?

—PAOLO VIRNO,
A Grammar of the Multitude

I DISCOVERED THAT THE MOST interesting music of all was made by simply lining the loops up in unison, and letting them slowly shift out of phase with each other.

—STEVE REICH,
Writings on Music, 1965–2000

every water
is the same water coming round.
everyday someone is standing on the edge
of this river, staring into time,
whispering mistakenly:
only here. only now.

—LUCILLE CLIFTON,
"the mississippi river empties
into the gulf"

10 Mississippi

1 MISSISSIPPI

The body recovered from the Mississippi River
this afternoon has been tentatively identified
as that of authorities on Tuesday identified
the body pulled from the Mississippi River
on Sunday evening as police on Saturday
identified a body discovered in the Mississippi River
this week as that of the crew recovered the body
of the man in the Mississippi River Wednesday night
and authorities suspect he may be the same man
bystanders witnessed enter the river Sunday
after several hours of searching the murky waters
of the Mississippi Tuesday night divers recovered
the body of a thirty-nine-year-old woman
local authorities pulled an unidentified body
out of the river's floodwaters Saturday
a body pulled from the Mississippi River
was identified Monday as that of the body
found last weekend in the Mississippi River
was identified Tuesday as that of a man from
the body of a man believed to be in his twenties
was pulled from the Mississippi River on Thursday
police said authorities are investigating after
a body was found inside a vehicle at the bottom
of the Mississippi the search ended Wednesday
after his body was discovered downstream
identification was released Friday night
of the man whose body was pulled from
Monday morning according to the sheriff
a body was pulled from the river.

Standing next to the river, I recorded the sound
of the river in an attempt to represent that sound
more accurately than my earlier description of it,
which compared the river sound to someone
saying "shhhh." I rewound the tape and played it back,
and the recording also sounded like someone saying
"shhhh," but then I remembered that I was listening
to both the recording of the river and the river itself,
and I could not with absolute certainty distinguish
one from the other. It sounded like the two sounds
synchronized into one "shhhh," but at times they
seemed to separate, as if telling each other to be quiet,
like accomplices committing a crime. Or they may
have both been telling me to be quiet, despite the fact
that I was producing no sound, or so I thought.
Retreating swiftly and quietly to the privacy
of my own home, a safe distance from the river itself,
I listened again to the recording of the river sound.
This time it sounded like a perfectly preserved memory
of the river, a solitary "shhhh" moving inexorably
toward the Gulf of Mexico, and just as I felt liberated
from the burden of having to remember the river
through my own mental activity, the recording stopped,
precisely at the moment when I had turned off
the tape recorder. Then I remembered that the river
itself was elsewhere, continuing its perfect sound
forever, and that I would never be able to represent
that continuousness accurately. I remembered,
however, that I could take a length of magnetic tape
on which that river was recorded and splice the ends
together to form a loop that I could then play

continuously. The sound could keep going "shhhh"
all the way to the Gulf of Mexico, telling all the cars
and condos to be quiet. It's worth remembering,
however, that a river is not a person, and that a person
saying "shhhh" eventually needs to stop making
that sound, either to inhale or die. There would be no
other choice, unless of course I recorded myself
saying "shhhh" and played a loop of that recording
continuously, in which case I'd no longer need
to remember myself. I'd be immortal
in the privacy of my own sound.

3 MISSISSIPPI

A drowning victim's body typically
sinks shortly after death. Typically
it resurfaces three days to three weeks
after death. Depending on a variety
of circumstances. Three weeks
of circumstances after a body sinks.
Before surfacing is caused. Bloating
causes. Surfacing is caused by
bloating that increases the volume
of a body. Without increasing
the weight. A body bloats.
An increase in the volume
causes. Bloating is caused.
Gas formations released
during putrefaction cause
bloating. Without increasing
the weight. Putrefaction is a stage
of the decomposition process.
Decomposition is caused
by death. Death causes.
Death is caused.

4 MISSISSIPPI

I saw a friend recently, I saw a friend I hadn't seen
in many years, I think we were glad to see each other,
but it was weird to see those years in each other's faces,
as if not-seeing could be seen, the creases around his eyes
and mouth looked like the distance between that last time
we saw each other and now, which was weirdly like seeing
me then and me now looking at each other there on his face,
which made our conversation weird, but we managed
to tell each other our stories about what we'd been doing
all these years, then I could tell he needed to tell me
something else, he said, can I tell you about what I saw
yesterday, he said, I was walking along the Mississippi River
and I saw all these people gathered, they were looking down
at the river, so I looked down and I saw a body floating there,
I saw this dead person just floating there in the river,
and he was totally naked, and he was huge like he weighed
four hundred pounds, or maybe he was just really bloated,
I don't know, and I could see in my friend's face
that he wanted me to see what he had seen, the creases
around his eyes and mouth quivered a little, as if they
wanted to reach out and take me to the river and show me
the body floating there, and I would look and I would
see the body, and I would wonder if it is the body
of someone I know or have ever known.

Foul play was not suspected, police did not
release further details including whether there
were signs of foul play, the cause of death
will not be known until the autopsy is completed
but foul play is not suspected, it's too early to say
how she died or whether foul play was involved,
authorities do not suspect foul play in her death,
we don't have any information to indicate
that foul play was involved but we haven't
completely ruled that out until we complete
our investigation said the sheriff, foul play
was not suspected in the death, all authorities
have been able to determine is that the body
is believed to be that of an adult.

Installed on the ceiling, the model shows the river mapped from the geocentric perspective, from inside the earth's interior looking up at the riverbed.
—JEN BERVIN, *Mississippi*

The continuity of abandoned courses of the Mississippi River and its tributaries can be clearly traced on aerial photographs where the scars of abandoned channels and associated features are discernible from the patterns of soils, vegetation and drainage.
—HAROLD FISK,
Geological Investigation of the Alluvial Valley of the Lower Mississippi River

Did we or did we not fly over the Mississippi then going to Minneapolis and St. Paul, I do not really know but if it was not then it was some other time where the Mississippi was a little river.
—GERTRUDE STEIN, *Everybody's Autobiography*

In all eight portraits, Betty wears a red dress, jacket or sweater, with white at her neck. Her latest rendition was created in honor of her 75th birthday, although she has hardly aged a day. Her hairstyles, clothes and demeanor have evolved to reflect the changing faces of American women.
—GENERAL MILLS CORPORATION,
The History of Betty Crocker

Because the course of the Mississippi River has changed a lot
over the course of its geological history, you might say that
there are many rivers in its memory, although these rivers
have never met each other, so gradually did they change
from one to another, never quite noticing the change
enough to say that a difference had taken place, the way
you don't notice changes in your face from day to day,
a new crease doesn't suddenly appear, and yet you might
say that you've had many faces over the course of your life,
you can even see them in photographs, you can study them
as a geologist studies changes in the earth in a photograph
taken from an airplane, you can come to know a photograph
of flying over the remembered rivers on your face, or choose
another face that everyone knows, like Betty Crocker,
everyone knows there is only one Betty Crocker and yet
there are many, it would be interesting to invite all the Bettys
to a party, they would probably enjoy meeting each other
and seeing the little differences between their faces,
how each one has a different set of creases, it would be
interesting how they keep asking each other, do I know you,
and of course they do, they've never met but they know well
what it's like to be Betty, that party would be historical,
and it would naturally give birth to other parties, if you
were a geologist you might have such a party, you might
invite many Mississippi Rivers, they would look like
many abandoned courses of the Mississippi River
seen in a photograph, they would look at each other
and be an interesting party of seeing little differences.

The first rule of hide-and-seek is that the hiders
must be given time to hide. Before seeking,
the seeker must count a sequence of numbers.
So as not to count too quickly, she must
repeat a multisyllabic word after each number—
1 Mississippi, 2 Mississippi, 3 Mississippi.
Initially, the seeker will resist the sound
of the word because it appears to be an obstacle
to her primary task of seeking the hiders.
To be a successful seeker, however, she must
understand that she is singing a song.
The four syllables of the word *Mississippi,*
each propelled by an *i* vowel, begin to slip
through her lips with a fluid sonority—
8 Mississippi, 9 Mississippi, 10 Mississippi.
She is flowing like a river, and the hiders
are following her to the Gulf of Mexico.

River, I don't know if you know what a baby is
but I swear there is one sitting on your bank
and even more amazing is that he's eating liver pate,
I know because it's making me gag a little
but somehow this baby loves liver pate on crackers,
this liver lover and I are looking at you, river,
and we don't know how you slither all mirrory
beyond our line of sight and yet like a screensaver
you never go away, you are always there, river,
almost rhyming with silver, but sadly nothing
rhymes with silver, and happily nothing rhymes
with something like a barge full of chickens
rhymes with finger lickin', like river rhymes
with sliver, and from outer space, moreover,
you look like a silver sliver stuck in the eye
of a chicken-faced world, the same outer space
you see in the mirror, like a good screensaver,
even when you get turbulent, river, I don't know
how you don't get tired with all that moving
but never going away, like a cadaver that keeps
moving, I mean there is nothing cadaverous
about you and yet you crave cadavers, I don't know
how you don't get tired of eating all those people
who fall into your mirrory face, and what about
the chickens, I don't know how they feel about
being eaten by a river, but if that is their destiny,
could you please remove their livers and give them
to the baby so he can eat liver pate forever,
he is quite a liver lover, river, and eating
all that liver will help him live forever
while sitting on your bank, while you eat
your cadavers like a good screensaver.

In bodies of water, dead zones are areas of oxygen depletion.
Dead zones cannot support life. The prime cause of dead zones
is an increase in chemical nutrients in the water.
This increase, known as eutrophication, causes the growth
of harmful algal blooms. Growth causes harm
when harmful algal blooms grow. When the algae dies off,
decomposition leads to low-oxygen conditions
known as hypoxia. The growth of algae leads to death,
which causes hypoxia. The most notorious dead zone
has grown to occupy an 8,543 square-mile region
in the Gulf of Mexico. The Mississippi River dumps
fertilizer and other high-nutrient runoff
into the Gulf of Mexico. The dead zone grows.
High-nutrient runoff comes from the vast drainage basin
of the Mississippi River. The drainage basin includes
the heart of agribusiness in the United States.
Agribusiness is the business of growing.
Agribusiness grows a growth known
as the Gulf of Mexico dead zone.
A growth business is one that expects
to keep growing. A dead zone is
a growth that cannot support life.

A police spokesman said the body
had been in the water "a long time"
and was "significantly decomposed,"
security video footage showed the man
at the lock and dam taking off his clothes,
scaling a security fence and jumping
into the river, her bike was found near
a hole in the ice, he left the party upset
and called a friend during his walk home,
in the last moments of the conversation
he cried out for help before the phone died,
two juveniles walking by the river
spotted the body, he might have floated
down from upstream and he might not,
said the sheriff, hours before he vanished
he appeared upbeat, her car was found
in the parking lot of the Pastime Lounge,
the medical examiner said he had tattoos
of a bald eagle on his right shoulder,
barbed wire with blood droplets on
his right biceps, a heart on his left forearm,
the river is a monster and people need
to be careful out there, said the coroner,
he disappeared after leaving his house
in a "manic state," according to authorities,
divers began searching for a possible
missing person after a frantic dog
was seen looking over a hole in the ice,
when responders arrived they found
a cell phone and gloves near the hole,
surveillance video from the bar

showed that the man took off his clothes
and stood as if he was about to enter
the water but was then pushed
into the water by the other man,
her body was pulled from the water
as friends stood nearby.

Five

Everything only connected
by "and" and "and."

—ELIZABETH BISHOP,
"Over 2000 Illustrations and
a Complete Concordance"

and every handout in every town,
and every lock that ain't locked
when no one's around

—ROGER MILLER,
"King of the Road"

Terminal Moraine

(AFTER DANTE)

Midway on our journey we'd gotten lost like golf balls
in a dark forest. Like tiny brains shanked into the unknown
by a slippery three wood, we'd forgotten why
we were supposed to keep score. One of us said,
up ahead there's a new path, let's give up the old path.
Soon the new path began to look like the old path in reverse,
and we kept feeling that old loss of newness.
Someone said that we were lost on the geological debris
left behind by a glacier 10,000 years ago,
midway on its journey back home. Someone recalled
getting lost once in a photo booth on a beach in New Jersey.
Someone recalled getting lost once in a bumblebee costume.
Someone said that researchers had put some ants
on stilts and cut the legs of other ants in half
to prove that ants find their way home by counting steps.
We'd lost count long ago, but then someone recalled
a small green pond at the start of our journey and said,
we should start thinking like a pond. The pond appeared
and said, this is the end of the path, you should start
thinking like a fire. Already we could see the burning wood,
and the trees all around, the not-burning trees,
watching the fire with awe. Someone said,
if you look far enough into the fire you can see
the embers flashing like a tiny chorus line.
Someone said, if you look far enough into the stars,
you can see a limousine pulling up, ready to drive us
into morning. The pond said, listen to these kick-ass frogs,
they remember what the glacier felt like when

77

it retreated, like it was letting go of a book
it would never finish. We listened to the frogs,
and for a while, we didn't say anything stupid.

Green Afternoon

We believe everything the grass tells us.
We sit there listening to the bad news.
There are no accidents. Oceans have no business,
ghosts have no feet. Someone had an accident
and was cut out of her clothes with special scissors
because of all the blood. They say it will be o.k.,
but that is a lie. Those pants will go to heaven.
Time will pass, and passing feels like swans
that no one can see. We watch the moon instead,
because it's free of charge. We conserve energy.
We hang laundry out to die. We let the neighbors
kill their kids. We watch the red-haired neighbor
burn her daughter's red pants in a Weber grill.
A matinee for the grackles and our cat, Monad.
Our self-evident cat watching the little flames
of where that daughter had inserted her body.
Our indivisible Monad who can kill a grackle
with one bite. We believe in quick death
and clothespins when the wind is blowing.
We believe the state flower is the lady's slipper,
and that Monad, a self-cleaning appliance,
will never die. We place him in our boat
and begin rowing through the green afternoon.
The more we row away from the grill,
the heart-colored grill, the closer we get to it.

The Whiteness of My Family

But not yet have we solved the incantation
of this whiteness
—HERMAN MELVILLE, *Moby Dick*

My brother the hazardous waste inspector
sent me a news report about a fire that burned
down a warehouse of white phosphorous
at a U.S. Army arsenal. In the news report
my brother said there's been an impact to creeks
in the surrounding area, contaminated water
made it to the river, and there was a fish kill.
My brother the inspector said his department
will continue to monitor the arsenal's clean up
of whiteness from the news. The arsenal said
a leaking can started the fire, but the fire
has been extinguished by the fish kill.
Many years ago my brother grew inside
our mother's uterus. He grew curious
and swam down the river and found the sun
that first burned his baby ass. He learned
his vowel sounds, he learned how
to speak of wasted rivers and leak
a can of painful news. The more I learned
from him, the more we sounded like each other,
the farther we swam, slurring our consonants,
rounding the bend, coming to the mouth.
The same mouth that said there's an arsenal
in the future, personnel are cleaning the slab
where the fire burned down the warehouse
of whiteness, but there's the possibility

of a flare-up in the future. When
our family lived in total whiteness
in a house wrapped in aluminum siding,
it was time to wash our hands, we were
about to eat dinner. Then my brother
dumped all the fishfood in the tank,
and the fish saw the ceiling of their lives
as too much eating to make it to the river.
The whiteness said it will get dark in the future,
and if you look into the dark far enough,
you won't remember what the stars look like.
Sometimes when you're underwater
they all begin to look like
one big star.

Slow Emergency

(AFTER JOHN CASSAVETES)

Here's what happened: you fell into the firepit
just like your father did, and your mother
kept walking circles around the house
not calling 9-1-1, saying I can't call 9-1-1.
She would not become a telephone
while another firepit death occurred.
She would refuse to watch fathers turn
to ashes because they had not yet learned
that flammable words are best,
whispered in the rain or the telephone,
long distance, far from the house.
Until then, fathers were doing something
to death and not knowing how to feel,
throwing themselves against garage walls,
acting in control of their shit until
their shit took the form of being lost
in another country. To get there,
they had to cross a lot of water,
they were thrown across it, trying to look
not worried, no sense being worried
in the middle of an ocean, things will soon
happen on a hotel bed in another country.
Here's the thing I'm going to tell you,
said the father, while the not-father
back home sat in the rain, watching
the not-rain come down. While the eye
of the firepit watched the house-shaped flame,
and your mother circled, not calling 9-1-1.
Weeping stucco of the father-shaped house

82

watching several ghosts thrown
against a garage wall, raining sideways
against it like watery lives projecting a film.
Ghosts who spend their lives waiting
for a heart attack, they sit outside
in lawn chairs talking about ice cubes.
There is a family of ice cubes melting
in a tumbler, and you can hear
what those little frozen oceans
say while losing their shape.
You can hear the sun killing them.

A Life of Consolations

You'll get your reward in heaven, said my mom
when I didn't make the cheerleading squad.
I remember this while pretending to study
the street map. Why do these little defeats
keep stabbing me after all these years?
I change. The light changes. I drive
up and down streets whose names
I don't know. I drive along the river,
curving with its curves. I still
can't do the splits. At times
I've had too many freckles.
I have an old snapshot of them.
Like stars at the bottom of a chocolate milkshake.
That would be a good way to die.

Among the Most Well-Educated Motherfuckers

I can't look at the snow fall without hoping for school to be canceled. My life depends on the radio angel saying we're going to get twelve inches on the ground.

I decide to run for governor so I can declare a snow day. Like a governor, I'm happy in a white mess. I'm lucky to have parents who are lost in the snow. My state is being wiped by toilet paper. My state makes a whispery song.

We make songs in music class. Everyone gets a little drum and we rub the skins with our fingers. That's the sound of snow falling. The trees listen. The branches collect the flakes who are afraid of falling all the way.

When the ground wants to get fat, it snows, and the more it snows, the less it hurts to fall on the ground. The fattest continent is Antarctica, and I'm running for governor of it.

Every day I have to eat, every day the school cafeteria serves a kind of meat. Except on snow days, where does the meat go then? Does it peek inside the incubator to see if the fuzzy chicks have hatched?

But not all the eggs can hatch. Some things die before being born, some die later. It's like a game show, me the contestant, the answer chicken salad.

My hat grows white feathers, I call it macaroni. I feel a little sick, my hat fills with vomit, I call it macaroni.

I have to go, so I go to the snowy hill. I use my favorite teacher as a sled. My favorite teacher is naked. I lie down on that pretty body, and we go, Yankee Doodle going to Antarctica.

But there's so much going that I begin to cry. My teacher forgives me and gives me an A, but I've already died of shame. I never go back to school. It never stops snowing.

The Rest of My Life

I have a little man on me.
His ear is pressed against my sternum.
I believe he is listening to my heartbeat.
As if it were important information,
the names of informants in a foreign city.
As if I were a hotel room he reserved.

Outside, there is a mathematical glow.
One by one, each airplane in the world
takes off, roaring overhead.
Passengers sucked into their seats
pause their anemic conversations
and stare into the space above row seven,
the same space I'm staring into.
It's like a huge form we're all filling out
on a clipboard, and there's a question
we don't know how to answer.
When was your last tetanus shot?

I have a little scar, but I don't know
where it came from. It looks
like a little man. He sleeps like
an emperor after an important feast.
He has burped and adjusted himself
for maximum comfort. I try not
to move, so as not to disturb him.
Have you noticed how hard it is
to be still? As long as my
heart keeps beating.

Free Will

In the warm red house across the street live two women
who are firefighters who are in love.
They have two happy red lions
who run in slow motion as if they're on fire,
always being saved by the firefighters.
Sometimes it's hard to know if anyone has ever
been saved or made a choice.
There are fires happening all over the world.
Many of them speak English.
There is a fire in Greenland
in honor of the warm drug that has eaten us for lunch
here in Kansas City.
When our mayor speaks, she sounds like
a warm drug, she says it's o.k. to love
a fire before fighting it to death.
What swims through our blood is the same happy red.
Since we live across from two bodies
who can swim into the fire as if it were a warm drug.
Since two lions watch us as if we were information,
it's hard for us not to be in love.
In Korea there's a fire
in honor of our Dwarf Korean lilac,
which we planted with love.
We dug a dwarf hole and made a dwarf hill next to it.
We climbed the hill and then let go.
Accidentally or by choice, we fell
into the hole and began to grow like a lilac.
Now we watch it grow, and the lions
watch us grow. My mother watches a show
about vaginas and she loves it.

She loves all the unborn daughters
who will grow up to fight the last great fire.
There is a fire in the Kansas City of my torso.
There is a solar plexus and no sudden rainstorm
promised by the radio. All the women
who love, they're fighting fire
on the radio, on the icebergs, in the words
that hate the water that drowns them.
The women who belong to each other
and belong to the water that drowns,
all the sleep that dreams a redder red,
and the oxygen that feeds it.
So we won't turn to ashes before
we make the choice to burn and be in love.
We sit back and watch the fire.
It is the English language,
and the lions are going to sleep in it.

The Religion of Sticks

1

Once there was a family of sticks, and these sticks knew how to bleed. They had a lot of blood to give, and every evening at the dinner table they passed a cup around and filled it. Then the father would lead the family in prayer to the one big tree from which they all came, and sometimes he'd tell a story about how everyone eventually dies, and how it is good to die a little every time you give the tree some blood.

2

I learned early on that blood would eagerly leave my body if I let it. When the big tree in our front yard died, it had to be cut down. Everyone gathered outside to watch, but I couldn't watch because I had a really bad nosebleed. Then I realized that if I tipped my head all the way back, I could watch upside-down, which made the tree look like it was falling up. In the years to follow we burned that tree in the fireplace, log by log. The flames reminded me of my nosebleed.

3

A letter came and I opened it with a sharp letter opener without realizing that I accidentally sliced my finger. The letter was from a carpenter ant, and he said that he'd like to be my savior in exchange for eating the firewood stacked in the backyard. The letter was signed, "yours truly, Jesus." That's when I realized that I was bleeding profusely.

4

The thing about sticks is, they're all born broken. They begin in original sin, which encourages them to form a small protective unit called "family." Every summer the carpenter ant returns and wants to eat more wood. Every evening at the dinner table we remind ourselves that there is never enough to eat, and that we should be grateful for what we have. My little stick heart keeps pumping my blood as far as it will go, then back again.

Why I Am Not a Bald Eagle

There should be / so much more
—FRANK O'HARA, "Why I Am Not a Painter"

I am not a bald eagle, I am a person.
Why? I think I would rather be a bald eagle,
but I am not. Well, for instance, there is a lake
in this city, and there is an eagle in a cottonwood tree
eyeing the lake. It seems impossible because
eagles do not like cities, especially skyscrapers,
but there he is, focused on the water as if
the city did not exist. I have never been that focused,
and what's really scary is that he doesn't seem to care
that I exist. I am neither friend nor enemy,
I am equal to seed fuzz drifting through the air.
His head is the whitest thing I've ever seen.
He is a very good looker. I think he is looking
for lunch, so I put the word "sardines" on him.
I think we both like the way "sardines" looks
on him. Moreover, he looks like my grandfather,
who ate a sardine and watercress sandwich every day
of his life and died of prostate cancer anyway.
I have not gotten cancer yet, fortunately,
and one day I am thinking of a color: white.
I imagine that if cancer were a color it would be white,
like the eagle's head. My grandfather, too,
had a cold temperament, unflinching and serious,
as if looking for something to destroy.
Pretty soon the whole sky turns white,
and on the lake's far shore, downtown rises up
like a bouquet of glass tumors. The tumors stretch
across the glassy water, they want to destroy

everything, but the eagle doesn't blink.
And one day I am walking around the lake again.
I see the same bald eagle in the same tree,
except that he no longer has "sardines" on him.
He doesn't look at me. It's like he doesn't
even know me, his own grandson.
It's like he knows that I am not
strong enough to love his cancer.

Six

THE ACTIVITY OF READING has on the contrary all the characteristics of a silent production: the drift across the page, the metamorphosis of the text effected by the wandering eyes of the reader, the improvisation and expectation of meanings inferred from a few words, leaps over written spaces in an emphemeral dance. . . . He insinuates into another person's text the ruses of pleasure and appropriation: he poaches on it, is transported into it, pluralizes himself in it like the internal rumblings of one's body.

—MICHEL DE CERTEAU,
The Practice of Everyday Life

BUT SINCE IN ANYTHING I HAVE WRITTEN, there have been lines in which the chief interest is borrowed, and I have not yet been able to outgrow this hybrid method of composition, acknowledgements seem only honest. Perhaps those who are annoyed by provisos, detainments, and postscripts could be persuaded to take probity on faith and disregard the notes.

—MARIANNE MOORE, "A Note on the Notes"

Variations on a Theme
by a Rooster

> *No barnyard makes you look absurd*
> —MARIANNE MOORE,
> "To a Prize Bird"

To hear the rooster doodle-dooing
at the end of the stinking alley.
To go there each time without going
because each doodle-doo sends
a video link of the rooster's red wattles
flapping under its erupting beak.
To travel down the alley lined
with life forms rotting in trash cans.
And to have said, I will text you
when I get there, I will tell you
that the rooster event is happening.
To have said, I will not stop to watch
eggs frying in a kitchen window,
I will not stop to watch the starfish
climb the dying Dutch elm.
My task is to go there to download
the doodle-doo, to see the saying of it,
and to say in response, thank you
for sending your flapping red wattles,
I enjoy your doodley discourse.
There is indeed a rooster not
far from here, and he happens
in quotation marks, and he happens
on the internet, and if this means
he has no barnyard, it also means
he looks less absurd because

he is not cow nor starfish nor
senator from the great state of
having a great-great-grandfather
who was once a poor farmer.
I am indeed anxious about what
it will feel like before it feels
like performing for the rooster
a farmer love song live on screen,
about saying to him, I am anxious
that you will deny knowing me
three times before you doodle-doo.
Already spring has denied me
three trillion times, and it is amazing
how deeply unknown I can be
while you get less and less absurd.
And as the stinking alley sends me
there to see the saying of you,
the rooster, wearing this city
like a new theory, like a cap
made of fleshy red fingers
pointing to your god, you will
deny knowing me, you will deny
knowing how to doodle-doo.

Random Violence

I found a bullethole in my room.
At first I didn't believe it.
I poked it with my finger.
I looked through it.
There was a bright circle of outside light.

Now when I leave my room,
I take the bullethole with me.
I go to the room where the gun lives.
Rather than knock on the door,
I enter through the bullethole.
The gun doesn't recognize me,
and I tell it that I have the wrong room.
But I see a letter on the desk
trying to explain: it was a dark night,
it was an accident.

Sometimes I take the bullethole to the moon.
I remember what my mother said,
that the moon is the mother of bulletholes.
I remember what the cop said,
that the shooting was likely a random act.
How often does something enter
your room without permission?

Sometimes I think I can see the shooter.
There is a face and a hand
in the window of a passing car.
The only light, just enough,
comes from the moon.

The thought of the act being random
brings a weird comfort,
I'm embarrassed to say.
I could've been here in this room,
as I am now, standing in the line of fire,
but I wasn't, and my absence
was no less random.

The bullethole gives me a familiar look.
We've been together for a few years.
I still haven't found the bullet.

Some Moons

Baby moon. Me moon.
Born in the morning see-thru moon
makes it easy to forget last night's moon.
Butterfly drunk on a lake breeze moon.
Little piggies glazed for sucking
pulled into a suck-hole moon.
It's 10:51 a.m. and there's a ghost donut
perched on a high branch moon.
This little piggy goes to the market
to be sold as a sausage patty moon.
Don't look too closely at the moon,
it will eat you for breakfast.
Little green leaves make little incisions
in the skin of the cheese moon.
Moon learning to be a little piggy
slaughtered slowly over a lifetime.
Don't forget the moon, it may forget you.
Remember to turn the moon into milk
before you get the no-milk blues
and drool a huge puddle moon.
Every song circling your bluesy baby lips
sung by a Bessie Smith moon.
A blue moon watches a big blue heron
shave the lake's skin without touching it.
Every good boy learns not to touch
the moon unless he wants to wet the bed.
A wet dog jumps into his warm dry sleep
from a ten million gallon moon.
It's 10:51 a.m. and totally awake
is the baby moon. Don't be afraid

to be made by the moon. Born to be
awake at this exact time under
a glow-in-the-dark wristwatch moon.
This is the time for a blue-winged piggy
who goes wee wee all the way
to the moon. This time it could be
any animal who once was a baby
born not drowning in drool,
there in the empty sky.

All Umbrellas Come from Fire

All flus come from China.
—DOBBY GIBSON, "Fumage"

Only you can prevent forest fires.
—UNITED STATES FOREST SERVICE

"Fumage" is a word that sounds French
and means "Smokey the Bear."
Fear of fire comes from the intense desire
to make fire. Thus, Wolfgang Paalen
invented fumage by drawing figures
on paper with the smoke from a candle.
They are sooty, savage humans
with sausagey limbs, dancing like bears.
Many bears are called "fumage"
because of the funny way they dance,
but only Smokey wears pants.
What's the function of those pants?
Only you know the answer.
The word "fumage" also refers to smoking,
as in smoked fish, and of course bears
are known to dance in exchange
for sardine treats. They participate
in an economy driven by scarcity.
Only you have what I want.
Each genus is divided into species.
All panda bears come from China
and are stuffed with flammable stuffing.
All stuffing comes from dreams.
All truths come from the flu,
curled up in bed in the shape of a moan.

When you look out a window at 2:47 a.m.
and the neighbor's garage is on fire,
it feels like you did it. Only you
are a pyro. Or a little after noon,
the sun pressing down on your neck
like a forest fire, and the angular shadow
that slips under your shoe each time
you place it a little farther up the sidewalk
is the one thing that comes from you.
It is your only idea, and if you
look away, it doesn't exist,
there is no idea that we come from
the smoke of a candle. And yet we know
that all umbrellas come from China,
and when it begins to rain there,
we open our umbrellas here.

Lecture on Kickball at Sundown

I was the keynote speaker, not the red ball kicker.
It was the child who kicked the ball, causing it
to roll through the green grass. As the speaker,
I wanted to be factual and natural in describing
how the young person swung a foot with great force
into the strawberry-colored sphere, not like
an old robot. It was classic kicking weather,
not snowy or smoggy. The ball glowed like
an old sun, and out in the field, a team of strawberries
played defense. It was a special game of kickball,
and I was the umpire squatting behind the child.
The strawberries were positioned rhizomatically
in the field. They were ripened to a deep red
embarrassment. The child stood watching the ball
travel across the planet. I said, you must run
like a president or the strawberries will eat you.
I could feel an itch blooming on my perineum.
I wore underwear that had been made in China.
I thought about how a Chinese person had once
touched my underwear. I looked at the strawberries
and saw little red satellites. The ball rolled over
the horizon. The child began to fade.

A Cat as King of the Fog

Then there is nothing to think of.
—WALLACE STEVENS,
"A Rabbit as King of the Ghosts"

Fog is a cloud in contact with the ground.
Fog begins to form when water vapor condenses
into tiny liquid water droplets in the air.
When fog begins to form, your mouth may
become very dry. You may be about to wake up
and see the fog and think of a glass of water.
To see the fog, you must be at a distance from it.
You must look through an ambitious window.
You are about to have an idea about what
to have for breakfast, and the fog is fuzzy mold
already growing on that idea. In this way,
fog is what eats your breakfast, and somewhere
in that fog your fat cat eats a baby rabbit.
In fact, cats like to kill, and fog is friend to killers,
but what thinks it is hiding is always being
watched by what hides it. In this way,
the fog watches your fat cat turn red as it kills,
but even this bright red you can't see,
even the red sign that begs everything to stop,
even the red lights of downtown have been eaten
for breakfast. You must therefore become
a believer, you must believe that in the fog
things still exist. There is a point which
has a corresponding antipodal point which
is diametrically opposite to it. Those two points
are connected by a line that runs through the center
of the earth like an elevator shaft through

an underground skyscraper. You stand
in the elevator not so much moving as being
moved, acted upon, and you have chosen
to push the one blank button. When the bell dings,
and the doors slide apart, you see that the fog
is still there even as you step into it. You feel
that the fog is for you, that somewhere
in the fog an accordion plays a song for you.
It's your birthday, and when you find the cake,
you must stab it with a knife so that you can
live another year. You must eat the cake
so that you can believe it once existed,
so that the fog will never need to reveal
something except the rabbit fur and bones
from which your cat stripped the flesh clean.
You believe that the fog is for you, but
the hardest thing to believe is that you
deserve it, and that there is nothing
to think of, just before it lifts.

Global Revision

Say the time of moon is not right for escape.
—LORINE NIEDECKER,
"When Ecstasy is Inconvenient"

At last, a chance to simplify.
As if we'd forgotten how to say
the dog was licking her body.
No, despite her ravenous technique,
she was not sweet. And yes,
the toddler did toddle
after an errant Ping-Pong ball,
disregarding national boundaries.
Some observers wondered whether
we had abandoned crawling too soon,
causing so much destruction
with confused little feet.
Years later we emerged from the clutter
like things we forgot we needed.
One of those retro labelmakers
that looks like a space ship.
It was a chance to put the word "bridge"
on a bridge, the word "there"
on where the bridge took us.
Without any irritable reaching
after the past, we had our own story
about the future. Nights already
getting cooler. Leaves turning gold.
The pleasure of cutting and pasting
daylight until the central idea
came into focus. There it was,
like a seagull without a sea,

without the need for a sea
to feel alive. Seagull perched
on the rim of a great empty goblet,
feigning a great calm.

Blueberry Island

All afternoon I've done nothing but sit on my ass
on a big rock called Blueberry Island.
I'm surrounded by thousands of wild blueberries,
and not one of them cares about my ambition.
They're bored by my fear of accomplishing nothing today.
This morning my ambition was to be the cause
of certain interesting effects, but I am making little progress.
10,000 years ago a glacier bulldozed
this landscape, leaving behind this craggy brain
lapped by 10,000 gallons of heaven juice.
I am trying to think about that, and how,
in comparison, my ambition is misguided and pathetic.
All I have done today is imitate lichen.
I cling to this island, not moving until my ass
aches so much that I have to shift my weight a little.
I try not to disturb a fly who has been walking all over me,
dragging its proboscis across my exposed skin,
sucking up some invisible nourishment.
Every now and then it stops to play a tiny stringed instrument.
I can't hear the song, but I can hear the purl of an eddy
down where the water meets the rock.
I am trying to remain outside of the fly.
Honestly, I am trying not to be boring right now,
but it is boring how much of my ambition has been an attempt
not to be boring. I have spent many hours gossiping
about the pain of others. Or I have selfishly
wanted to be alone, afraid to be known.
There is no special boat coming to get me.
My ass sits on a 10,000-year-old migraine headache.
Jack pine and juniper have twisted into fantastic positions.

An orchid's fuchsia lobe glows like a tiny casino.
Soon I will have forgotten all of this.

THE COFFEE HOUSES of seventeenth-century England were places of fellowship where ideas could be freely exchanged. In the cafés of Paris in the early years of the twentieth century, the surrealist, cubist, and dada art movements began. The coffee houses of 1950s America provided refuge and tremendous literary energy. Today, coffee house culture abounds at corner shops and online.

Coffee House Press continues these rich traditions. We envision all our authors and all our readers—be they in their living room chairs, at the beach, or in their beds—joining us around an ever-expandable table, drinking coffee and telling tales. And in the process of this exchange of stories by writers who speak from many communities and cultures, the American mosaic becomes reinvented, and reinvigorated.

We invite you to join us in our effort to welcome new readers to our table, and to the tales told in the pages of Coffee House Press books.

Please visit www.coffeehousepress.org
for more information.

COLOPHON

10 Mississippi was designed at Coffee House Press, in the historic
Grain Belt Brewery's Bottling House near downtown Minneapolis.
The text is set in Minion with Scala Sans for display.

FUNDER ACKNOWLEDGMENTS

Coffee House Press is an independent nonprofit literary publisher.
Our books are made possible through the generous support of
grants and gifts from many foundations, corporate giving programs,
state and federal support, and through donations from individuals
who believe in the transformational power of literature.

Publication of this book was made possible in part, as a result of
a grant from the Jerome Foundation. Coffee House Press receives
major operating support from the Bush Foundation, the McKnight
Foundation, from Target, and from the Minnesota State Arts Board,
through an appropriation from the Minnesota State Legislature and
from the National Endowment for the Arts, a federal agency. Coffee
House also receives support from: three anonymous donors;
Abraham Associates; Allan Appel; Around Town Literary Media
Guides; Bill Berkson; the Patrick and Aimee Butler Family
Foundation; the Buuck Family Foundation; Dorsey & Whitney, LLP;
Fredrikson & Byron, P.A.; Jennifer Haugh; Anselm Hollo and Jane
Dalrymple-Hollo; Jeffrey Hom; Stephen and Isabel Keating; Robert
and Margaret Kinney; the Kenneth Koch Literary Estate; the
Lenfestey Family Foundation; Mary McDermid; Deborah Reynolds;
Schwegman, Lundberg, Woessner, P.A.; John Sjoberg; Charles Steffey
and Suzannah Martin; Jeffrey Sugerman; the Archie D. & Bertha H.
Walker Foundation; Stu Wilson and Mel Barker; the Woessner
Freeman Family Foundation in memory of David Hilton; and many
other generous individual donors.

This activity is made possible
in part by a grant from the
Minnesota State Arts Board,
through an appropriation by the
Minnesota State Legislature
and a grant from the National
Endowment for the Arts. MINNESOTA
STATE ARTS BOARD

TARGET.

To you and our many readers across the country,
we send our thanks for your continuing support.

Good books are brewing at www.coffeehousepress.org